SEA CUCUMBERS

by Wendy Perkins

AMICUS HIGH INTEREST • AMICUS INK

Amicus High Interest and Amicus Ink are imprints of Amicus
P.O. Box 1329, Mankato, MN 56002
www.amicuspublishing.us

Library of Congress Cataloging-in-Publication Data
Names: Perkins, Wendy, 1957- author.
Title: Sea cucumbers / by Wendy Perkins.
Description: Mankato, Minnesota : Amicus High Interest, [2018] |
 Series: Weird and unusual animals | Audience: K to grade 3. | Includes
 bibliographical references and index.
Identifiers: LCCN 2016038826| ISBN 9781681511603 (library binding) |
 ISBN 9781681521916 (pbk.) | ISBN 9781681512501 (ebook)
Subjects: LCSH: Sea cucumbers--Juvenile literature. | Marine animals--
Juvenile literature.
Classification: LCC QL384.H7 P47 2018 | DDC 593.9/6--dc23
LC record available at https://lccn.loc.gov/2016038826

Photo Credits: tets/Shutterstock background pattern; Manfred Bail/
imageBROKER/Alamy Stock Photo cover; orlandin/Shutterstock 2;
treetstreet/iStock 4; Michael Stubblefield/Alamy Stock Photo 7; Mark
Conlin/Alamy Stock Photo 8-9; Georgie Holland/age fotostock/Alamy
Stock Photo 10-11; Klaus Stiefel/Flickr 13; Masa Ushioda/SeaPics.com 14;
Alexander Ogurtsov/Dreamstime.com 17; para827/iStock 18; cbimages/
Alamy Stock Photo 20-21; Ria Tan/Wild Singapore/Flickr 22

Editor: Wendy Dieker
Designer: Aubrey Harper
Photo Researcher: Holly Young

Printed in the United States of America

HC 10 9 8 7 6 5 4 3 2 1
PB 10 9 8 7 6 5 4 3 2 1

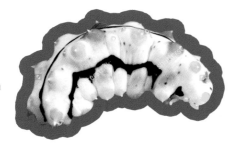

TABLE OF CONTENTS

4

AN OCEAN VEGGIE?

A sea cucumber sometimes looks like a vegetable. Some people even eat it. But it is an animal. These long, soft animals live all over the world. You can find them at the bottom of the ocean.

SMALL AND BIG

Some sea cucumbers are long.
Some are round. Some kinds of
sea cucumbers are no bigger than
your thumb. Others are as long as
a grown human.

7

SUCKER POWER!

A sea cucumber has hundreds of little **tube feet**. They work like suction cups. They grip rocks and the seafloor. Some tube feet are around the mouth. They are for grabbing food.

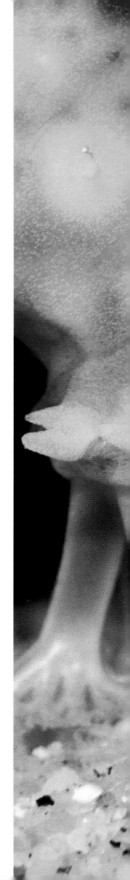

9

FINDING FOOD

Some sea cucumbers crawl to find food. Others stay in one place. These kinds bury most of their body in the sand. They have long tube feet around their mouth. They catch tiny plants floating by.

CLEAN-UP CREW

Some sea cucumbers eat sand and mud. The stomach takes away little bits of food. Clean sand comes out of the animal's **rear end**. They help keep the ocean floor clean.

13

14

ON THE MOVE

Some sea cucumbers swim by bending their body back and forth. Others push off from the bottom and then sink back down. They catch bits of food as they fall.

WEIRD ENDS

It is not hard for this animal to breathe and eat at the same time. It eats at the mouth end. But it breathes by taking in water through the rear end!

FAT OR THIN

A sea cucumber can change its shape. It can make its body look big and fat. It can also become very thin. Then it can slip between rocks to hide. That's a good trick!

20

A MESSY TRICK

The sea cucumber has another trick. It spews out its **guts**! This scares away **predators**. The guts are covered with a sticky liquid that stings. Ouch! Later, it grows new guts.

A LOOK AT SEA CUCUMBERS

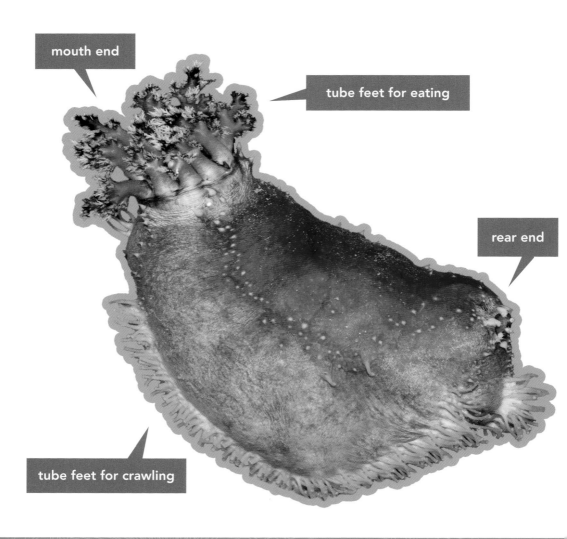

mouth end

tube feet for eating

rear end

tube feet for crawling

WORDS TO KNOW

guts – body parts that are inside and work to digest food

predator – an animal that hunts another for food

rear end – the part of the body where waste comes out

tube feet – body parts that are shaped like a straw and use suction to grab things

LEARN MORE

Books

Rake, Jody S. *Sea Cucumbers*. North Mankato, Minn.: Capstone Press, 2017.

Schoeller, Jen. *Biggest, Baddest Book of Sea Creatures*. Minneapolis: ABDO Publishing Company, 2015.

Websites

Aquarium of the Pacific: Sea Cucumbers
www.aquariumofpacific.org/onlinelearningcenter/species/johnsons_sea_cucumber

National Geographic: Sea Cucumbers
http://animals.nationalgeographic.com/animals/invertebrates/sea-cucumber/

INDEX

Every effort has been made to ensure that these websites are appropriate for children. However, because of the nature of the Internet, it is impossible to guarantee that these sites will remain active indefinitely or that their contents will not be altered.